11/18

How to Find Information Online

by Amanda StJohn
illustrated by Bob Ostrom

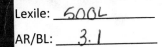

The Child's World®

Published by The Child's World®
1980 Lookout Drive • Mankato, MN 56003-1705
800-599-READ • www.childsworld.com

Acknowledgments
The Child's World®: Mary Berendes, Publishing Director
The Design Lab: Design and production
Red Line Editorial: Editorial direction

ISBN 9781614732518
LCCN 2012932865

Printed in the United States of America
Mankato, MN
July 2012
PA02127

About the Author

Amanda StJohn is an author and public librarian.
She's fascinated by singing frogs and animal tracks
and enjoys apricot tea and knitting.

About the Illustrator

Bob Ostrom is an award-winning children's
illustrator. His work has been featured in
more than two hundred children's books and
publications. When Bob is not illustrating children's
books you can usually find him in a classroom or
online teaching kids how to draw.

Spring was a magical time for Opal Owl and Stew Rabbit. They liked to play in puddles after a heavy rain. They also liked to help Opal's mom plant flowers in the garden.

One day while watering flowers, Stew saw the peonies shake. "Whoa!"

"Shh!" Opal whispered. "Something is hiding in the peonies!" Then she crawled beneath the peony bush and disappeared.

When Opal came back, she seemed to be carrying a rock with legs. "It's a tortoise!"

"I call that a turtle," replied Stew.

"Will it eat my peonies?" asked Opal's mom.

Stew stroked a whisker. "My dad thinks turtles and tortoises are the same thing."

"Remember what our teacher said about what people think?" Opal asked.

Stew smiled. "What people think is called an opinion. Sometimes we want facts."

"Right," agreed Opal. "Facts means truth."

Opal looked at the animal she was holding. "Are you a tortoise or a turtle?"

The animal didn't answer.

"Stew, it's library time!" exclaimed Opal.

They grabbed their helmets, hopped on their bikes, and they were off. They arrived at O'Hare Public Library in no time.

Opal and Stew walked into the children's section of the library. Miss Mantis, the children's librarian, waved hello.

"Miss Mantis, we have a question," said Opal.

"Are a tortoise and a turtle the same thing?" finished Stew.

"What a good, clear question," said Miss Mantis. "This sounds like a great question to **research** online." She led Opal and Stew to the public computers. Opal and Stew knew they should only go online when an adult was there to help.

The three sat down, and Opal opened a Web browser. A **search engine** appeared.

In the search engine, Stew typed: "Is a tortoise a turtle?"

Stew's search offered many results. Opal clicked on one of them and a new window opened. It said, "Buy a turtle now!"

"Whoops," said Opal as she closed the window. "That doesn't answer our question."

Stew clicked the next result. The title read, "A Tortoise Is Not a Turtle: A Blog."

"This isn't right either," said Stew. "A blog is someone's online journal. It's someone's opinion. For research, we want facts."

"Miss Mantis?" Opal asked. "Are we doing something wrong?"

Miss Mantis smiled. "Are you using a search engine made for kids?"

Opal and Stew looked at the search engine. It didn't say "for Kids." It had a plain white background. The kids' search engine they used at school was more colorful.

"No," answered Opal.

"How do we find a search engine for kids, Stew?" asked Opal.

Stew remembered something from class. "Go to the library's Web site."

In the search box, Opal typed: "O'Hare Public Library." She found the library's Web site. "Look! There's a **link** here for a kids' search engine."

Miss Mantis said, "Very good, you two. The library's Web site is a helpful tool."

Stew typed in the kids' search engine: "Is a tortoise a turtle?" A list of Web sites appeared. The very first Web site was all about turtles and tortoises. The first sentence said, "A tortoise is a turtle that lives only on land."

"Wow!" Stew gasped. "Is that true?"

Miss Mantis said, "What do we do after we find some answers?"

"Check the **source**." Opal was so excited her feathers fluffed.

Miss Mantis nodded, "The information must come from a good source, like a university or an expert. An **encyclopedia** is also a good source."

Stew asked Opal, "Do we know who wrote this?"

"No," said Opal. "There's no author listed."

Stew wondered, "Then, do we know who put the information online?"

"Look at the bottom of the screen," helped Miss Mantis.

Opal scrolled to the bottom of the Web site. "It says 'O'Hare City University.'"

"Great!" Stew exclaimed. "Last, we make sure the information is not too old."

Opal pointed to the date. "2011. That's new."

Opal and Stew danced about. They knew they had found a good source online. They read the rest of the **article** and learned that most turtles live in wet and watery areas.

"Awesome!" said Opal. "Is our work finished?"

"I want to find one more source," said Stew.

Opal was confused. "Why?"

"Because," Stew crossed his arms and smiled. "If this information is true, another source will say the same thing."

Opal and Stew returned to the search results. Opal read the titles and picked "Turtles and Tortoises." They checked the author and the date. They decided it was a good source.

Opal and Stew read the "Turtles and Tortoises" article. They learned that turtles and tortoises are related.

Opal pointed at the screen, "It says right here—'Tortoises are turtles that live on land only.'"

"Look!" Stew found a picture in the article that said: "Painted Turtle."

Opal's eyes widened. "That's it! Our garden animal is a painted turtle."

"Excellent!" said Stew. "We answered our question!"

"Thanks, Miss Mantis!" chorused Opal and Stew as they left the library.

Opal and Stew rode their bikes back to Opal's house. They were going inside when Stew remembered something.

"Didn't your mom want to know if turtles would eat her peonies?" asked Stew.

"Oh," cried Opal. "You're right. Let's look it up on the computer."

Opal and Stew waited for Opal's mom to join them. Then they went to a search engine for kids.

"Okay," said Opal's mom. "Let's start with a question."

"Do turtles eat peonies?" Opal decided.

In a search box, Opal typed: "Do turtles eat peonies?" But the search engine did not show any information that answered her question.

"Sorry, mom. I guess we'll never know," sighed Opal.

Stew didn't want to give up. "We could try to search for a different word. We can try 'flowers' instead of 'peonies.'"

"Do turtles eat flowers?" Opal typed. Again, the search engine found no results that answered the question. Opal and Stew whispered together about what to do.

"We could pick a different search engine," Opal said.

Then, Stew's eyes lit up. "What if . . ." he began.

Stew continued, "What if we ask what turtles eat?"

Opal liked Stew's idea. She typed: "What do turtles eat?"

At last, they had results. Opal and Stew clicked one open. The Web site was an article in an encyclopedia.

"Turtles eat insects, fish, and plants," read Opal. "Plants?"

"But do they eat flowers?" Opal's mom asked.

"Oh no," cried Opal. "This says some turtles like to eat flowers!"

"Roses, pansies . . . " read Stew. "It doesn't say peonies."

"Let's check another source," smiled Opal's mommy. "The expert . . . the turtle itself."

Everyone hurried to the garden. The peonies were still there, but the turtle was nowhere to be seen.

Stew said, "It may be an opinion, but I'd say this turtle does not eat peonies."

Glossary

article (AR-ti-kul): An article is a short piece of writing usually found in newspapers, magazines, and encyclopedias. Opal read an article about turtles.

encyclopedia (en-sye-kloh-PEE-dee-uh): An encyclopedia is a book or set of books with articles of detailed information about many subjects. It can also be online. Opal found information in an encyclopedia.

link (LINGK): Link is short for hyperlink. It is a clickable word or phrase that takes you to a new Web page. Stew clicked a link to an article online.

research (REE-surch): You do research to learn more about one topic or idea. Stew did research about turtles.

search engine (SURCH EN-jin): A search engine is an online tool that finds information on the Internet. Opal used a search engine to research turtles.

source (SORS): A source is a person or business that wrote the information you found online. A university is a good source for information.

Tips to Remember!

- Always use search engines built for kids.

- Check your library's Web site for kid-friendly search engines and information.

- Look for facts, not opinions, when doing research.

- Choose information written by experts or universities.

- Choose the most recent information you can.

Web Sites

Visit our Web site for links about library skills: childsworld.com/links

Note to Parents, Teachers, and Librarians: We routinely verify our Web links to make sure they are safe and active sites. So encourage your readers to check them out!

Books

Halpert, Ben. *The Savvy Cyber Kids At Home: The Family Gets a Computer*. Atlanta, GA: Savvy Cyber Kids, 2010.

Jakubiak, David J. *A Smart Kid's Guide to Doing Internet Research (Kids Online)*. New York: PowerKids Press, 2009.